PIANO • VOCAL • GUITAR

BON IVER  A MILLION

ISBN 978-1-4950-8351-8

HAL•LEONARD®

Visit Hal Leonard Online at
www.halleonard.com

Contact Us:
Hal Leonard
7777 West Bluemound Road
Milwaukee, WI 53213
Email: info@halleonard.com

In Europe contact:
Hal Leonard Europe Limited
42 Wigmore Street
Marylebone, London, W1U 2RN
Email: info@halleonardeurope.com

In Australia contact:
Hal Leonard Australia Pty. Ltd.
4 Lentara Court
Cheltenham, Victoria, 3192 Australia
Email: info@halleonard.com.au

22
(Over Soon)

Words and Music by
JUSTIN VERNON

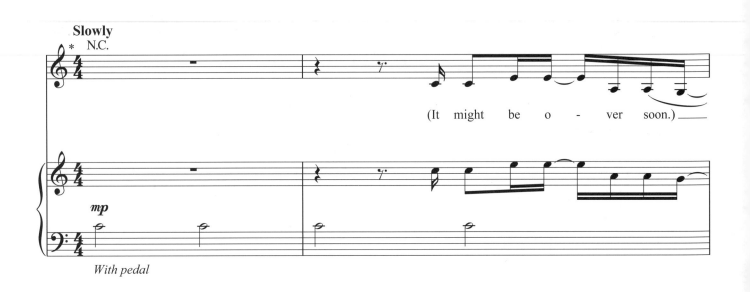

(It might be o - ver soon.)

(Soon, soon, ah.)

(It might be o - ver soon.) Where you gon-na

Recorded a half step higher.

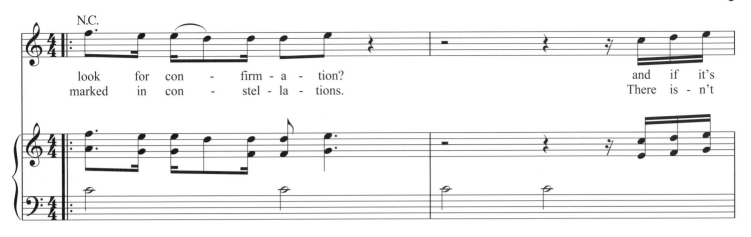

look for con - firm - a - tion?
marked in con - stel - la - tions.
and if it's
There is - n't

ev - er gon - na hap - pen? _____
ceil - ing in ____ our gar - den. _____
So as I'm
And then I

stand - ing at ____ the sta - tion,
draw an ear _____ on you

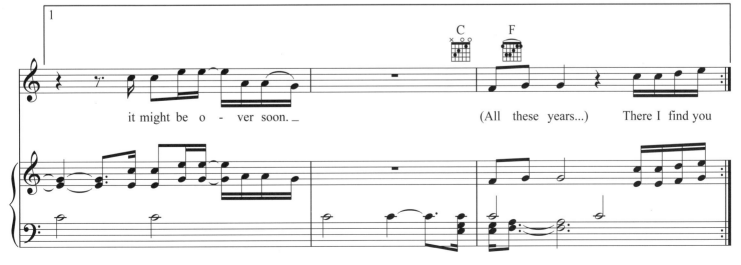

it might be o - ver soon. __
(All these years...) There I find you

Solo ends (That I'm-a shine

one more time, Lord.) Oh, and I have car - ried con - se - cra - tion;

and then you ex - pelled all de - ci - sion.

As I may stand up with a vi - sion...

caught day - light; god - damn__ right.__

With - in a rise, there lies a scis - sion.__

(It might be o - ver soon.)__

715 - CREEKS

Words and Music by
JUSTIN VERNON

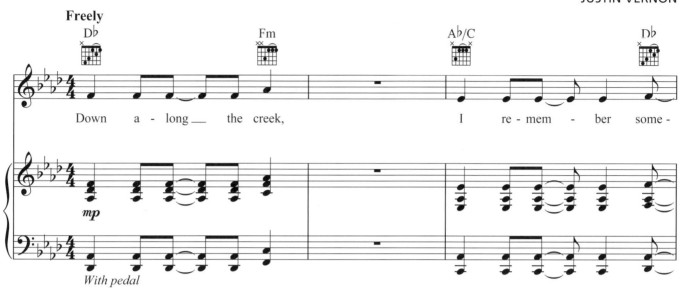

Down a-long__ the creek, I re-mem - ber some -

- thing... Her, the her - on hur - ried a - way__ when first I breached that

Tempo I

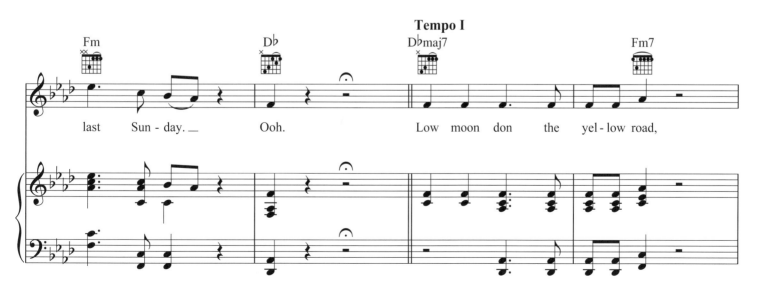

last Sun - day.__ Ooh. Low moon don the yel - low road,

10 dEAThbREasT

Words and Music by JUSTIN VERNON,
BENJAMIN LESTER and BRANDON BURTON

* *Recorded a half step higher.*

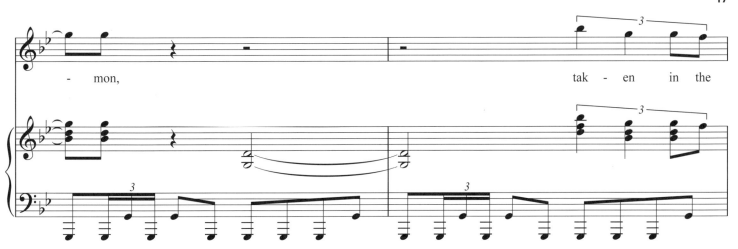

- mon, tak - en in the

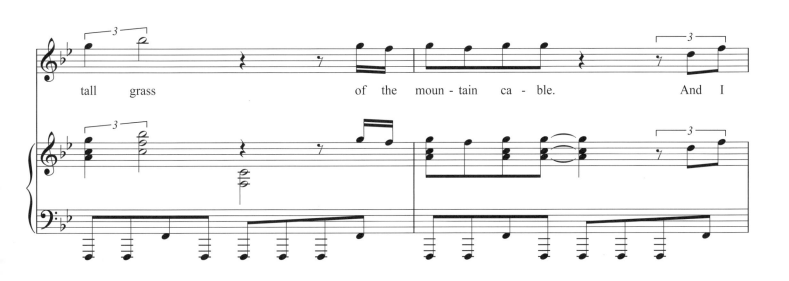

tall grass of the moun - tain ca - ble. And I

can - not seem to find I'm a - ble.

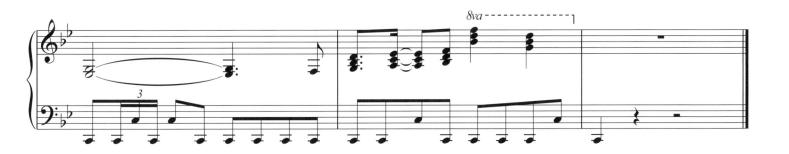

33 "GOD"

Words and Music by JUSTIN VERNON
and WILLIS GRAHAM

(Here in this room, this nar-row room, ___ where life be-gan, ___ when we were

young once, I...)

Well, we walked up on that bolt in the street, af - ter you

tied me in in the drive-way of the a - part - ment of his bede...

29 #Strafford APTS

Words and Music by JUSTIN VERNON
and BRANDON BURTON

666
(upsidedown cross)

Words and Music by
JUSTIN VERNON

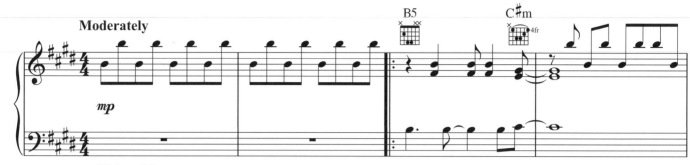

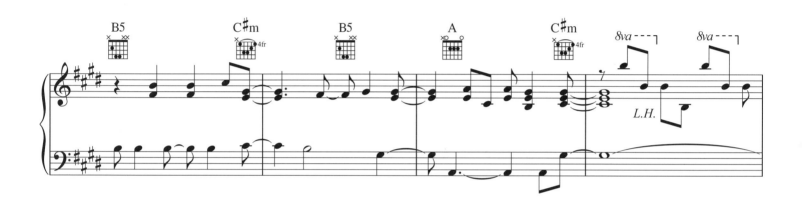

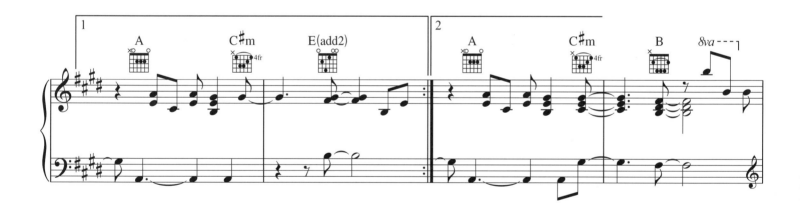

8 (circle)

Words and Music by JUSTIN VERNON,
RYAN OLSON, BRANDON BURTON
and MICHAEL LEWIS

Recorded a quarter step higher.

42

21 MOON WATER

Words and Music by JUSTIN VERNON
and SEAN CAREY

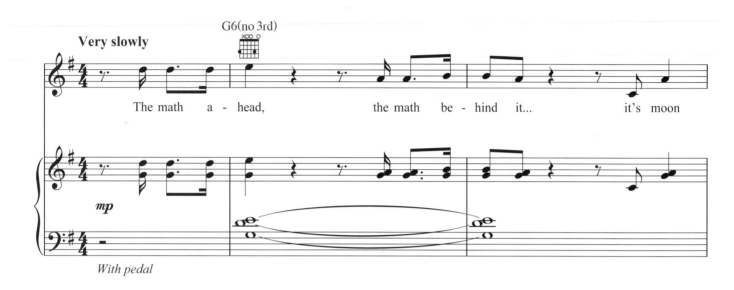

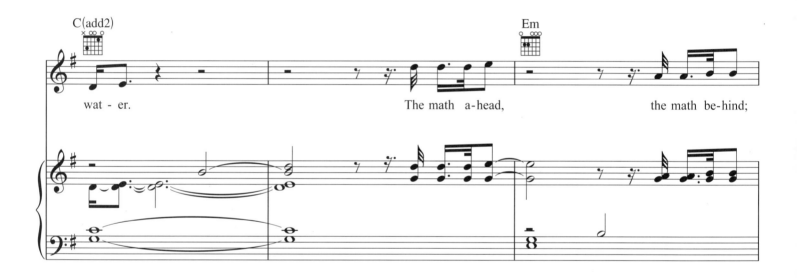

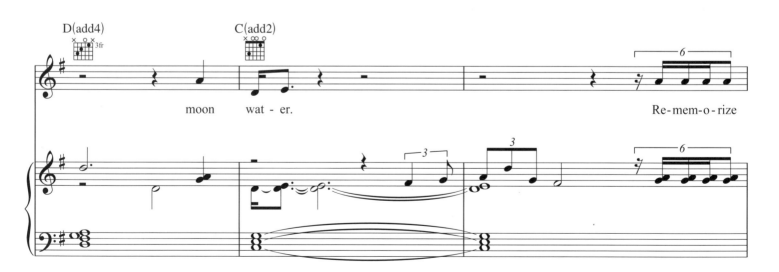

00000 Million
(1,000,000 Million)

Written by JUSTIN VERNON,
MICHAEL LEWIS and FIONN REGAN

__45__

Words and Music by JUSTIN VERNON
and MICHAEL LEWIS